ST

TIMING

ANNE ROUSE

TIMING

BLOODAXE BOOKS

ISBN: 1 85224 404 6

First published 1997 by
Bloodaxe Books Ltd,
P.O. Box 1SN,
Newcastle upon Tyne NE99 1SN.

Bloodaxe Books Ltd acknowledges
the financial assistance of Northern Arts.

Cover printing by J. Thomson Colour Printers Ltd, Glasgow.

Printed in Great Britain by
Cromwell Press Ltd, Broughton Gifford, Melksham, Wiltshire.

for my sisters
MARY, KATHY *and* ELIZABETH

Acknowledgements

Acknowledgements are due to the editors of the following publications in which some of these poems first appeared: *Bad Moon Rising, London Magazine, The Times Literary Supplement* and the Big Wide Word Poetry Bus (Route 38, London). 'Testament' first appeared in *Poetry* (Chicago).

Seven of these poems were published in Maura Dooley's anthology *Making for Planet Alice* (Bloodaxe Books, 1997).

I'm grateful to the Authors' Foundation for their considerable support, and to Wesleyan University, Connecticut, for a scholarship to their 1995 Writers' Conference.

Contents

Hotel Mundo

The hotel offers
sixty rooms over traffic;
one bath, in a scum of suds,
and its cracked brother.

The Irish cleaner
enquires each morning
if I am leaving, but it is
out of my hands, this matter.

The woman slanting
into her hairdryer, the old
man-and-stick, the pale
young thing – I tell them,

Hotel Mundo belongs to you!
– The missing drawer-knobs,
the taps like green stalagmites,
even the darkened mirror.

Raising the first alarm
along the line of cells,
I warn them: there is only
one flaw in our distress –

A small drift
of joy, trying the air
in the light swirl of steam
from a visitor's cup.

Testament

To my last technician,
I leave this flaming skeleton.

I like you better
than a doctor, or a hairdresser.

My leaving do's a blast, a whirl,
I'm a party girl,

Nude and ablaze like a tree,
one spectacular x-ray.

Look up from the gauges, be a voyeur,
a happy pyro-connoisseur,

But don't think to make free
with the calcine ash, the grit of me –

That's for a feeling hand,
or the wind.

The Anaesthetist

This rubber pump in my hand sighs, pants, and wheezes
for you, my dear. Nighty-night, Ms Prynn.
Forbuoy approaches to wheel you in.
He is the theatre orderly. He *is* theatrical,

whipping off the dark green sheet like a tablecloth,
leaving you with nothing much to fall back on.
You are well under now, a gleaming cold matron.
Forbuoy is messing about with his pink slop.

The surgeon pulls latex over his finger joints;
the nurse displays her swift knives and forks.
Forbuoy and his shadow start to snigger, the oiks,
in the holy second of waiting.

The present, powerful, naked Ms Prynn
glows and is bold, illumined further
by the big lamp lowered like a flying saucer
as it hovers, stops.

Then round that star-lit table we are all drawn in.
You are turned and covered; your back basted pink.
I touch your wrist, while you stumble in your Hades walk,
Ms Prynn, at the first, sharp rocks.

Dosser

Those eyes are dust, that were blue flame;
your trousers blackened, on you since the Flood.
The walkers swerve around you. *Gissa quid.*

You're camped under the Body Politic –
chat-show head, arms dealer prick,
Soho snatch and Bow Street anus –

You're the shit, an affront
to the eyes of the old citizenry,
and to your old disputant.

You're the sleeper on waste ground.
Things have worked out differently for us.

Woman, 28, hung for stealing a watch

It belonged to a father of the city.
I had a child with me; he did not do the stealing.
I thought it should belong, like luck, to me.
At the thought of time, they lay down frantic sheaves
on marble mantel-piece and round clock-tower,
but I've known her steady as the flux of moons.
Her voice is quickening; immeasurable.
The child died. I am not pleading hunger.
The watch described the gift of time too woodenly,
as she walks down the river steps with me,
and I carry the child into those, sweet waters.

£5 Haircut

No cup of tea, no blow-driers, no *conversazione*,
no lacquered bobs shining from magazines.

Buzz-cut young men step up one after another.
My head is pushed into the penitent position.

A hairshirt begins its wheedling under my collar,
as the silver shears divest me

of the human, which, flittering to the base
of the clinical chair, heaps softly.

The Mayo Man

He was fighting it, he didn't want to be in that story:
the one that started, *the Mayo man had a nasty fall*
after a night's hard drinking,
so we carried him up, me and Sean, to the hospital
when the night shift had glided out through the swing doors,
with their brollies and cardigans.

Powdered and pink and bare as a washing glove,
in his bottle sleep, his roaming,
until the day a nurse leaned over softly
to find that his dry lips moved:
Where would you be going like, I says.
Would that be any of your business now, he says.

The Mayo man relating his best home yarn,
if it could have ended there:
how he'd trudge up and down the long corridors,
frightening the visitors with his shaved, solemn head;
grinning the once, when the boys came in to the dayroom,
passing a hip-flask along a tight ring of chairs,

shoulders touching, glancing shifty behind.
The poor man had nothing whatsoever to say for himself.
Sent home at the finish to Mayo.
Queer in the head, they can do nothing for him.
Mute, between escorts. *Now don't be forgetting this.*
Your story. O Mayo Man, tell it there.

Bella Dora

Bella Dora, a patient at the Institute of Calm,
used to look too long at the sun.
She wanted to go blind, she said, troubling the nurses,
so that someone will take care of me.
Round-eyed, she stood among the parked cars and seemed,
with her head tipped back, to be drinking sunlight.
When her wealthy family flared onto the ward
she followed them demurely,
but she wanted to age into their imperious marshal
with a white baton, their shadow walking before them;
to demand love, to accept it without shame.

Star

I raise my forearm against the lens and they never get me.
Paparazzi stunts, hack sermons don't matter – or didn't
until the *döppelganger*, an LA shark dead-ringing for me,
started bluffing his way into Le Caprice or Jerry's.

This guy had a past, teen-aged girls, other rumours,
to wreck a White House soiree, drop the sponsors in Swanee.
I took some advice, the palmist, the clinic, a Monterey lawyer.
I tracked this jerk down a restaurant alley: wrong I.D.

The guy who turned around with a frown was a third man,
a fan, who wore my twenty-year old face on his t-shirt.
Then I saw the glint of the piece. Do you know who I am,
I asked, but his eye was exact. Point-blank, in fact.

My twin copped it too and it's him they remember.
I'm in limbo, safe, where no one knows me. Many mansions –
forget it, this is more like a cell, lightless
and senseless, but private: oblivion. The way I like it.

Shroud

You hold up this cotton gift,
but it's too skimpy for a dress.
It wrinkles like a windy lake, no style.
I've already got dead to carry, eaten furs;
I want a satin moment; a twirl of joy.
If this dolour suits you, wear it,
but my blood's gone chic and scarlet,
and I make small-talk like a deb,
murmuring, live or die.

Newsvendor

Blonde – Buxom – Bewitching,
I offered French polish
to city gents, in the 60s.

Their brusque sons encounter me
as a blue-haired old doll in a kiosk,
flogging breath mints and the FT.

The fury passes. They are merely cross.
Diaries and trains can make them sweat –
not love lost, or teasing sweet.

I guard a temple that is bare.
They peer out, shaved and grim,
from safety's cage.

Interloper

You bask, and look about like a crowned prince.
Over you dragon-flies stitch and re-stitch.
The margins rise to condense a greeny dank.
You're the unwanted love, voyager:
you might enrich the mud, but you've nosed too far
in the lapping swill, and the algae's net.
The consequence is barbed, and urgent.
Taste it, and know death.

Queynt

Hostage to the phalli,
where are your celebrations?
In the delivery suite;
among the porn queens?

Blood-warm and sea-brine,
maroon luxurious
rupture, your monuments
aren't theirs,

columns and Concorde; you've
only you, strong
as grass, sly mouth. Lewd
old thing.

Sex in the Culture

Sex in the culture
is drug & liberty bell.
I knew its guises,
both stern and cheerful,

but then with you, that hour,
cut off from the mainland, normal day,
entirely, so I can't remember
what god could have spoken to us or why,

I felt unlike me, afterwards,
in every cell,
while downstairs you whistled and made tea.
It wasn't sex, not sex at all.

St Malo

I'm on the rampart walk tonight.
The body is like this stone-bordered city:
plundered, blank-eyed, windswept.
Strangers inherit it, *le corsaire*.
No honest sailor risks a howling sea;
or these rocks, fast against
the thirty-foot winter breakers,
and the thunderhead, blotting out the dawn.

The Cage

I am only meant to be the body,
and the other she that converses,
the clattering marionette,
stiff with lines the world rehearses.

But the burned she shudders in her cage,
and eats a hand that was forgiving,
gnaws it because she has no other food
and it insures the accident of living;

and in her flayed extremity can't know
if it is her flesh or her keeper's,
who wants her hot and black as toast,
and as mute as sullen sleepers.

If her shrieks rose up as words,
they'd soothe and put the fire out –
her keeper wants her warming for himself,
and so she thrashes dumbly on the spit.

Timing

Light hosanna'd in the mirrors.
We were double, multiple; but our quadrille
ended when you bowed and faded.

This evening in you walked – foot-sore, apologetic.
A minstrel, out of tune.
The sun had gone in, the room was brown

through the rattan blinds,
and I'm no coy languisher, no Penelope.
I'd done my scribbling in the book of you.

Pick-up in Soho

Hassan, who exhales the cologne of discernment,
whose cashmere coat could have graced Lord Lucan –

offers 'nice time' – wine-lit confidences interrupted
by the waiting flat, the hard relief of the animal.

His body hectors him to live; in a moment he'll be
back on the clock, upstairs with the New Blonde Model,

who welcomes up to six men an hour.
It's straight-forward here. I miss my lover.

Goodbye, and nice time, Hassan.

Talkers

I've met two kinds of talkers.
The one has undoubtedly suffered –
call it a birth trauma that lasts
seventy, eighty years.
Even the matter of which bus to catch
hurts them, they must talk it out.

The other isn't certain if they themselves
are real, but the mind, at least,
is a fountain, reaching and flourishing
when anyone nudges the pump-switch –
a caretaker, say, who at once discovers
in what profusion lonely love abounds.

Blitz

'In '41 it got so bad
every city morgue was full.
We couldn't unload our lot,
burned most of 'em, poor
buggers, and fragmentary.
We had to stack 'em in the dugout,
on the high bunks.
I sat on a cot while Archie
boiled us up three mugs, brown
as boots. Then a near hit
rocked the joists.
That one rattled us,
Bev the driver, Archie and me –
you could hear the bones jar
against the wood,
and the spoon jingling
in the sugar billy...'

At the Library

Although clever enough, and a reader, he
is our pent embryo, and we're his slattern mother:
those he knows he only knows
as warming scattered voices, who recite
an answering pleasantry, until pressed to follow
the backways of his thought: how X was rude
and what might be the reason, do you think,
(the reason coiling harmlessly round him)
and when I see him, pink and happy enough
in confab with a restive colleague, my old faith
in the object, mineral love veining human-kind
shudders, troubled at its source. Oh, he terrifies.

Leaf

Whorled and buckled
in the bawling sun, it turns
as brash as carnival,

staining itself cerise,
baroque and charred,
uncurling from the vine,

it eddies through nets of green
to a summer ground, heaped
with flames that have aged and ended.

Highbury Fields

It was VE day.
The beacon shrieked at the god of war,
this is what we do for excitement here, okay?

The coconut shy, the Chinese noodle treats,
the Crooked House for Kids, the mayor's
rites of torch;

pensioners in razzle hats, the conga line
of red-gold faces, and this flame
nattering at the sky for us –

Then a man with a grievance hurtled towards the fire.
Children and grown-ups craned in a ring
to watch running, cursing firemen

snatch him from the flames; bundle him off unsinged
to broadcast calming voices –
but we'd seen, and drunk. War had won.

Dawn

I met her with a hand to her lips,
hair riled and matted, fingers stained.
She rolled a slender fag from some leavings;

asked me again where she was. I tried
to say where but she hunched her shoulders
in the donkey jacket, which was too big.

Everything's too big for her.
The street light grilled us, chemical yellow.
She's away.

The Narrows

May I ask you a question?
A taxi driver to the mirror overhead.
What is there beside work and sleep?
The cab lolloped over a speed bump.

Pleasures go by and then we're old.
We slowed to a dieseled stasis.
Cab and man were shades of black,
handing me a Xeroxed sheet,

THE PURSUIT OF HAPPINESS.
I read it, leaning in at the meter light.
I can't remember what it said.
He was running the narrows quite alone.

I didn't have the nerve to tip.
With that muttering ease of cabs,
he drove off to confound another soul,
turning right on the station road.

Sunday Morning

Blood sprouts like early spring
among the styrofoam burger cases and butt-ends
of the Seven Sisters Road.

It was Saturday night, swearing
and uplifted, who sent these vivid notes
to Sunday morning, its shrivelled twin;

a red path ending in the sturdy daylight,
when he rouses,
only to ache, and smile.

Chanty

He only wants it when he's drunk,
the blowsy boy, the ligger man,
and then he barely sees me straight,
the raging rough inebriate,
and its heads or tails whether he can.

He hugs the armchair at his worst,
snoring and diagonal –
but if he's keen then down we flop,
and when the milkfloat whines we stop,
the drowsy boy, the devil man, the darling rascal.

The Hen Night Club's Last Supper

Take this bread roll and this
Sangria cup in remembrance that we
are one another's blood,
and come from women's body.

Drink, and eat tonight, my chucks,
in solidarity,
for dawn affrays with bloody men
in their obstinate beauty.

Go bravely into the world of snooker halls,
Downing Street and the packet of three.
Nil carborundum, bless the Marks,
and bless this company.

Spunk Talking

When men are belligerent or crude,
it's spunk talking, it's come come up for a verbal interlude:
in your face Jack, get shagged, get screwed, get your tits out,
get him, lads, bugger that, hands off, just you try it,
you're nicked, left hook, nice one Eric, hammer hard,
shaft him, stitch that, do you want to get laid or not, red card.
Spunk speaks in gutterals, with verbs. No parentheses.
Spunk's a young con crazy to break from Alcatraz.
Sonny, you'll go feet first. So spunk has to sing,
hoarsely, the *Song of the Volga Boatmen, I am an Anarchist,*
the Troggs' *Wild Thing.*
Cynthia Payne said, after her researches, not to be debunked,
that men are appreciably nicer when de-spunked.
Before time began the void revolved, as smooth and bored
as an egg, when a tiny ragged crack appeared,
and the world exploded like an umpire's shout,
as the primal spunk of the cosmos bellowed OUT.

Recall

The woods were casting shadows
when we kicked our sapling teepees down.
The squaw ran home; the neighbours began
their nightly mysteries.
I untied a clavicle string of groundhog bones,
and rubbed off the lipstick lines of war.
I can't hear the hot voices now
that call and call: I'm years gone,
at play in the alien grasses.

Creek

We followed the creek's intent.

The heckling water dropped
into the lit spas
of crayfish and green moss;

into the light high runnels,
and the pools, the stagnancies
of ink-black leaves,

and ran on
as a moving watchfulness
among frail trophies,

that lost their beauty as we walked
the trodden field;
drying in our small, enclosing hands.

Skirmish

They crouched, then ran, had to,
over the shards of cold along the creek,
ducking ricochets that flicked up scars of sap;
then they were running like deer, exchanging shadows
through the baffled smoke to Shenandoah.

After the real peace, they climb the ridge:
dusk, he leans against the lichen.
This time he drinks, not much, his hand fumbling
at the moss. They cut the dogwood wide,
to let his eyes take in the open sky.

Fairyland

The Christmas shoppers slammed and revved
in the K-Mart parking lot.
We handed up our quarters to the barker
for FAIRYLAND,

a caravan in mauve and lilac;
and wandered through
a doll-sized kitchenette
to a living-room in beige, immaculately scaled.

Someone had worked hard on it.
Maybe the little man in his undershirt,
who slumped and stared at the Japanese portable.
His midget wife was ironing with a toy.

She scowled, looking down; her eyebrows meshed.
We were only three gaping small girls,
who stumbled together, in a hurry,
and set out cold across the night's

unblessed and thorny wood, where now,
real wolves seemed to howl, and witches
worked an unfathomable spite.
Our footprints merged in the snow.

The Bluff

She'd never been here before: a bluff high
over the Accotink, where it surged with rain.
In the headlights she could make out an oak;
a rope, knotted and frayed like a mare's tail.

The boys she'd met jeered each other on.
She'd jeered at herself, but pictured it: swinging
back into the torchlight, too afraid to drop;
or breaking on a welter of rocks, like another stone.

'*Don't,*' one of the boys said. He hadn't jumped.
'*It's too dangerous. Don't.*' Another cry whipped
the blackness, then a deepening splash.
He was saying he'd drive her home –

along a country back-road, and down a rutted drive,
where she got out and he stared ahead,
white and cold, gunning the engine, and she
watched the climbing, faltering red lights.

Tree

The lights flicker in the depths of the fir tree,
signifying an idea of heaven;
from branch to branch flinging out necklaces:
neural, giddy, ecstatic.

Only a day ago quietly nurturing the forest,
felled, and borne off in ropes
to preside as the bedecked guardian of this house,
the tree accepts our tokens,

as if we could condense our intricate, fretted relations,
the silences, the out-dated news,
into these dazzling skeins: on, then on,
all night they flicker.

Hagiography

Her first poem, and a vial of blood.
It has been authenticated,
and the saline tears in that large dish.
Some visitors drop a coin and make a wish.
Can you hear me at the back? – this is
our lovely Statue with the Moving Eyes.
Over the years, many have claimed to hear it laugh.
Hans Lerder wrote the monograph,
(on sale next to the iced cakes in the Bleak Café)
describing some peculiar noises when the coaches drive away.

Jean Rhys

The defendant was unsteady on her feet.
'I am a West Indian and I hate the English.
They are a bastard mean and dirty lot.'

Rhys on the highway at Holt.
Her appearance was dishevelled and her breath
smelt strongly of spirits.

'I am Much Disliked.
Titles of books to be written, ten years hence,
or twenty or forty or a hundred:

Woman an Obstacle to the Insect Civilisation?
The Standardisation of Women, the
Mechanisation of Women, Mysogyny...'

The witnesses had thrown cold water over her.
'– well call it Misogyny – Misogyny
and British Humour will write itself.'

Laura Riding

One morning in her dominion, on the little isle,
she saw a mild and devious stranger
patrolling there,

the harbinger
of the dishonest great,
his pockets stuffed with rhyme.

She retired south,
to grow oranges that other poets tasted,
in a silence that swelled; that became itself a poem.

On the Holloway Road

Where then now, Jack Kerouac?
Down some reeling American valley
to Denver city;

San Fran Hoboken Mexico; old Jonah
in the sweltering gut,
bleached with a million fishes – ?

Come to the Holloway Road
Jack; you & any angels *en passant*,
the Roman Great North Way,

rich in wizened rubbish sacks,
furtive Greek card games; two or three
fast fooders, with TV zap and shine;

burrow in the velvet pubs of Celtic fiddle swing,
join the Secular Society and the Merchant Seamen;
circle the centrepoint of language

for zanzibars of meaning in this grey,
hero of sensations. Descend
to our foggy east, reddened with Dharma light.

Air Ambulance

They came running to the creature
cogitating on the hill. A man had fallen
from a window, but they weren't here for blood.
A policeman easily cleared the stretcher's way.

Strapped-down and red-blanketed, he'd
brought them their luck: this whirling visitant
that steadied itself, conferred,
and lifted above the glorious noisy wind;

that tilted, took on the rights of air and shot
itself as from a cross-bow, cleanly south. Far off
it looked the thing it was. They drifted back,
for tea and tv, nearly emptying the park.

The Dementia Ward

They're hunched under a hurling wind,
aslant in the foam-rubber chairs,

a round-robin meeting whose agenda is sleep;
or shuffling as far as the laundry room door,

intent on ancient purposes.
Dermot, there are books in that bag for the train.

I can do you bacon and egg.
Abandoning safety, careening like sailors:

Maude, gaping at the male assistant
with a crass, ineffable joy.

The Meditation

I descended into the whirling sea-black of the body.
They'd been complaining
about the head and its unquiet messages –
the neck and throat in particular were weary,
upholding, like Atlas, the coral cities of the brain.

But as we spoke, the head began to transcribe,
above us, like a steady planet,
a circle on the axis of the spine;
permitting its by-ways to gleam
into the night of the body; inviting them proudly up

to its 3-D wide-screen scented 8-track feely
cinema-cum-planetarium – but they had other preoccupations,
such as peristalsis, and breath;
they demurred, but I responded, and rose into that glitter again,
but it was dimmer now, its dubbed cries softer,

and I was well for a time.

Cigarettes

Brand X, the brand
of habitual beauty
– the wrist-flicked match,

the airy signature,
plush o's of smoke –
marks the man

that closest family visit,
with grapes,
and twenty Bensons in a purse;

who'd been greedy for nothing
exotic, like the real
Golden Virginia –

just local pleasures,
round the block.
Those little trips.

Lantern Journey

I was tiny and perfect
until time unfolded me,
rudely reversed its origami,
to expose an eye, then an ear,
to the feverish mirrors
in the splendid and terrible room
where I swelled, blue globe,
with every crease expelled and smoothed,
until time discovered a stick and beat me,
piñata, for the candies.

So they fall, in showers,
gorgeous and reliably fatal,
out and beyond the I,
its airy verdict collapsed,
its tatters unfurled,
until there is no line left
between me and the world.

Bleeding Hearts

These blooms in their party frocks,
they have no responsibility.
They tippexed it out.

Blood whitens to pink, their colour.
Mistakes for them are beads
on the bruising heart.

It was a tired act, an accident.
I need to shout it
at the sea, old winking Romany.

Let the long waves absolve me.

Egg

This is the thing to hunt in the Easter grass.
On the eye it is merciless,
red and hard like a tuber – or nothing at all,
a cicada's carapace.

It has taken a life to prepare,
like the golden Fabergé the poor goose died to inherit.

I want it shattered:
a yellow smear and a spot of blood
from which the lean cockerel grows, can still grow,
feathering its cry.

Thaw

You tease us, charmer.
AWOL for weeks together,
when the brusque Siberian complains.

But settling to warmth, we
marvel at your leniency,
your entrance braceleted in light.

Then everyone alive's your advocate.

Hello!

There's something gruesome about celebrity.
'Mr Red Star and Ms Violet La-la are taking tea
in their spectacular perspex inglenook, among the live fish.'
The lucky caul went to them, the clover and the genie's wish,
but the look-at-me breed seems as sodden as *papier maché*
with the humdrum blank witnessing of every press day.
They should hide, or go mad; as it is they go soppy,
and blur like the last-in-a-thousand photocopy.

An Apparition

She might have been
the angel militant,
speaking broad country,
red-haired, in ripped chain mail:

'It's an eden, enclosed
by a lake of water,'
her plain report, 'and love is
sips of that water.'

Lilies of the Field

You want corporate woman I get her for you
living doll on that billboard you like?
she got nice silicone, taped up brown eye shadow cleavage
skin by Max Factor and air brush
don't kid yourself even lights out she's a peach
spend how you like you may get her lay her
the modern world anything possible
telling your limerick on chat show
mama crying forgive her
and baby doll sucking her big eyes on you
da da   buy buy

Play On

Football and poems
are grace and havoc.
Pure attar of futility.
Nothing can come of it.
Nothing. I love that.

The kit is blood-red,
the substitutions ruthless,
the heroes French, or Celt.
A hydra-head roars
at their blazing backs:

the lines exultant, loping,
as they pass, and re-pass –
but there is one man, one
vexed and critical eye,
their nemesis.

Nevertheless,
they run, as if
their sensual, streaming
argument could persuade
that worrier to leap aside

from the nets of sense,
and watch them send
his beaten envoy home
on a green field;
in the grace of one poem.

Report by a Commission on Violence

Give every man a very sturdy dog.
Give babies tambourines that they can jingle.
Give generals clay armies; every hanging judge a mistress,
and every child a doll that she can mangle.

Give young men a bull with which to wrestle.
Give women punch-bags featured like young men.
Give bus conductors shields and lovers gauntlets,
set guards on streets and ban adrenalin.

Make mine a cocoa. Horlicks? Yeah, cheers mate.
Give up the car, the TV and his bed.
Become a vegan, study Buddhist chant,
and sleep, sleep, sleep until you're dead.

Returning to the Park in July

In April the goslings scattered
across the pavement – pell-mell
golden gusts of alive – where? gone
to low-slung, stately geese
poking about in muck like weekend royals,
or disembarking from the lowest dockside
kerplop, and gliding, beaks to the air,
assured, and never again astonished, never
fleeing to the shade and back between
the iron railings and the pond.

A Novice and a Childless Woman

Hugging a prayer-book, scurrying into church;
remote, in glasses and the nun's grey wimple.
The peace, of no.

The peace, of not.
Slim back turned on a hungry road. Head bowed.
Body bowed like a question,

until the answer comes to her entire.
She won't be raffling off her tenderness in numbered jars,
man after man. She may please her god today;

among the prowling shoppers there's one
of nature's tired acolytes,
where no rain falls. Who does not prosper.

Two Birds

There were two dead birds,
featherless young,
on the garden bricks this morning.

They were cold and blue –
but even so distrait, those
rude embryos

refused, with open beaks,
to enter the black plastic sack.
The earth will make

something of them.
She's the fecund one.
Why can't I be her handmaiden,

instead of writing out
these frail receipts – why not locate
my little plot, and live on it?

The Outlands

I've been walking the outlands of the self,
recording its cold impasses and its wounds,
its mudflats and fervent suns and thrashing water.
Someone had hung out bangles on the stunted
trees over the wallows. I nearly sank bejewelled –
then headed north-west to where the howls subside
at zero, and the moon loses its smudged nimbus.
Where I hear of remarkable cities.